101

Questions & Answers About Investing

A Guide to Help Beginners on Their Journey, Including Every Question I Had When I Started!

Mike Hartley

Disclaimer Notice:

The presented work is strictly informational and should not be interpreted as an offer to buy or sell any form of security, instrument, or investment vehicle. Furthermore, the information contained herein should not be taken as a legal, tax, accounting or investment recommendation given by the author(s) or any affiliated company, employees, or paid contributors. In other words, the information is presented without considering individual preferences for specific investments in terms of risk parameters. It is general information that does not account for a person's lifestyle and financial objectives. It is important to note that no tailored advice will be provided based on the given information.

The authors and their parent company, along with all employees and paid contributors, have agreed to abstain from trading any stock or investment written about for at least two days publication of any new article, book, report, or email. This includes any equity, options, debt, or other instruments related to that security, stock, or company, except for existing orders that pre-existed the submission; all such charges will be disclosed inside the document. The author(s) may have direct or indirect positions in some of the companies mentioned because of holdings in mutual funds, exchange-traded funds, closed-end funds, or other similar vehicles. Such indirect holdings are usually not disclosed as there is no guarantee that the author(s) is aware at any given time of the individual portfolios of any of these funds. Furthermore, certain decisions by these funds, such as buying or selling stocks, could potentially impact an author's position even if it was not done directly by them.

Warning:

There is no simple, easy way to become wealthy, especially regarding investments in the financial markets. While it may be possible to make a significant return on your investment, there is also a high risk of losing a large amount of money if you do not have the proper knowledge and knowledge base. You must conduct thorough research and analysis to succeed with investments with the most significant potential for price appreciation. Investing wisely requires an extensive level of education and an understanding of how markets work for one's portfolio to yield positive returns over time. Before venturing into any investment endeavor, it is essential to consult an experienced financial advisor or professional who can advise what steps should be taken and how much capital should be invested. It is also necessary to review all relevant information about potential investments, such as the company's financial statements and prospectus, to make an informed decision regarding whether to invest. Everyone must remember that past results are not necessarily indicative of future performance, so it is wise never to invest more money than you can afford to lose.

This work is based upon a thorough analysis of SEC filings, current news events, interviews, corporate press releases, and knowledge obtained through our experience as financial traders, investors, journalists, and educators. We encourage readers to be careful when making decisions involving their finances, as they are ultimately responsible for the outcomes of their choices. To ensure they have thoroughly informed themselves before making any investment decisions, we strongly advise readers to take the time to research each subject in more detail by seeking out additional sources such as third-party analysts or other reading materials on the web. Furthermore, we recommend conducting a comprehensive review of all available data to ensure each conclusion is well-rounded and sound by exploring multiple aspects of an issue or topic. Ultimately, we believe that a person's financial future will benefit from making prudent and informed decisions based on knowledge gathered from various sources.

The author(s) and any parent companies may be affiliated with certain investments offered. If any of these affiliate offers are made, it will be clearly stated, however, that such affiliation exists. It is worth noting that we do not, and would never, affiliate ourselves with companies that do not meet our high standards and ideals; we would not promote anything that we wouldn't consider ourselves, and in that vein, we aim to keep any affiliations with companies that we believe to be of considerable value to our readers, subscribers, and fans. We value your time and education and try our utmost only to offer the highest quality support.

All trademarks, whether registered or pending, are the property of their respective owners.

Foreword to the Series

Investing is a necessary and invaluable life skill that many people don't even realize they need. It allows you to create financial stability, accomplish your most ambitious goals, and secure your future. Whether it be providing for loved ones, avoiding the need to work past retirement age, or funding a dream vacation in Japan, investing requires a deep understanding of the principles of finance as well as those of self-discipline, patience, and sound judgement, free from any emotion or prejudice. While this may feel intimidating at first glance, investing can be extremely manageable with the right guidance and strategies that minimize risks while maximizing returns. By staying informed and educated on the basics of investing, we'll have you on the road to financial success.

Whilst this series masquerades as a comprehensive set of educational guides to the various inroads of investing, it is in fact a chronology of what I have learnt over the years - and from almost every aspect of investing there is. Growing up in a family that had relatively few financial resources, I was always driven to make something of myself and ensure the future security of my loved ones. One of the ways I set out to do this was by ambitiously aiming to make a million dollars in cold hard cash - which seems almost comical when I look back on it now as I had no idea why I chose this figure! A million dollars was just an arbitrary number that I decided upon when I didn't fully comprehend what it meant, or how life-changing it could be. I just thought to myself "I think having a sum of money would really help my family along", so, with this goal in mind, I began researching and investing in various different fields; from stocks to bonds to real estate to swing trading, and so on! My journey has been far from easy, but every step along the way has been incredibly rewarding as I've continued to learn about investing and building my wealth. Now, whilst making money is still a priority/hobby for me, having time with my family is what really matters - and is ultimately more satisfying than reaching any arbitrary figure.

Once I had achieved my goal of amassing a million dollars, it was not that such an amount was not enough; on the contrary, it is certainly a significant sum, and having so much money at once gave me a feeling of great accomplishment. However, I found that I didn't want to stop there. It wasn't just about wanting to make more money; it was about wanting to keep on experiencing the joy and sense of fulfilment from investing. As a youth, I had the dream of being rich and financially free, but with more experience, I now invest because I've learnt to love it! After sixteen years of engaging in this activity, I had finally come up with a system which enabled me to make consistent wins with most forms of investing. So, I figured, why should I let this newfound understanding go to waste? Why should I stop now when things were going so well?

When I decided to start learning about investing, I made sure that I was as prepared and organized as possible. I researched thoroughly, making notes on who offered the best services, the cheapest rates, and which brokerages had a reputation for being trustworthy. As someone who is naturally meticulous, it only made sense to take an in-depth approach to this as well. So, I made sticky notes, wrote in journals, and took copious notes in Word documents - all with the intention of compiling my thoughts throughout the process. Fast forward sixteen years later and here I am writing a series of books based on my experiences!

To ensure accuracy when writing this series from different perspectives - such as in 'Investing for Women' - I asked friends and fellow investors for their input to add further insight into each book. In fact, much of what is written regarding investing has been pre-written by me over time in various forms - be it a scribbled note or a more detailed outline of what I personally needed to know to invest in that field. Although not an expert in all areas of investment, through years of research and experience (and help from others!) I have been able to piece together content that reflects a diverse range of perspectives within this field.

Overall, this series of books is an amalgamation of much of my own research and experiences - some of which I have been continuing the entire time – others of which I've found either not profitable, or only mildly profitable, and so I've ditched them in favour of the better-earning ones! I have also included the thoughts, opinions and input from others involved in the investing world, to ensure accurate representation from a variety of perspectives. It has been a fun journey putting together all the pieces and rewarding at the same time. I am excited to share my knowledge and insight into investing with you all.

This series of handbooks provides a comprehensive guide for even the most beginner investor who is looking to start investing with confidence and ease. Each book dives deep into different aspects of investing, providing readers with the essential knowledge and information they need to make smart decisions when it comes to managing their money. These books are tailored specifically for those who want to gain a better understanding of investing in the financial markets and successfully managing their portfolios over time. Despite my American-based viewpoint, anyone can follow the principles explained within these pages regardless of their country. By reading this series from beginning to end, readers will be equipped with all the key tools necessary for success in investing and achieving long-term financial independence.

In addition to straightforward advice on how to invest, this series also offers guidance on everything from basic stock market terminology to more complex financial instruments. Readers will learn about diversification, risk management strategies, cost/benefit analysis, taxes related to investments, and more – giving them a strong foundation of knowledge that can be applied no matter what type of investment they choose.

My goal is for readers not only to understand what's going on in the markets but also to gain insight into why certain strategies have been useful for me, and how you can find the ones that suit you best.

Note:

I'm often asked what investments I'm presently making and it's an important question for those who are seeking to find financial freedom. After giving the matter a great deal of thought, I felt writing this information down in a book would quickly become outdated since I tend to rebalance my investments at least every three months. To provide readers with more up-to-date information, I decided to create a website which will help them understand what I am doing and encourage them to do the same. This website will not only provides details of the investments but also includes facts and figures that illustrate how these strategies can help people achieve their financial objectives. It will offer guidance on how to make wise investment choices and gives insight into the kinds of risk associated with each decision. Furthermore, this website contains detailed advice on how to maximize returns by diversifying your portfolio across multiple asset classes, mitigating losses through careful analysis of market trends, as well as other long-term strategies for achieving financial independence. By taking advantage of all the knowledge provided on this site, readers can feel confident that they have taken steps towards attaining their own financial freedom.

The journey to uncovering the secrets of successful investing can seem daunting, but I'm determined to make it easier for you! By subscribing to my email list, you'll stay up-to-date with the latest books in the series, and eventually be the first to know about my unique investment system. By being on the e-mail list I will also let you know when the website is launched too – exciting! I am constantly thinking "I wish I'd had this when I started! I'd have saved a decade worth of time!"

So, no matter your level of financial literacy, I have comprehensive information for anyone who is keen on learning more. With an array of resources at my disposal, I can give you an in-depth look at the foundation of successful investing. Through these materials, I will provide a thorough look into elements such as risk management principles and best practices, financial forecasting, budgeting techniques, and so much more.

On top of this knowledge base, subscribers will also be given access to exclusive tools such as calculators and other interactive features that can help simplify complex topics like portfolio construction. This way, no matter what your individual goals are when it comes to building wealth through investments - I'm here to help!

By joining my email list you'll have access to all these resources and more. So come on board for this exciting adventure and discover how you can get started investing for success today!

So, with no further ado, let's dive in!

Your Free Bonus Gifts

Accelerate Your **Learning**

Maximize Your **Earning**

We are here to help you crush it – no bones about it. To make the most of this book, there are two things you'll need:

1. **FREE RESOURCES**

   We have created a number of free resources for you to take advantage of. Use them to accelerate your learning and maximize your earning!

2. **FURTHER RESOURCES**

   We are constantly striving to continue supporting both our team and our students. We are busy creating a website to better highlight all of our investing tips, tricks and current holdings to help our users better see what we're actually up to! To find out when we launch this, and be alerted when we release other titles, just subscribe to our e-mail list and you'll be the first to know!

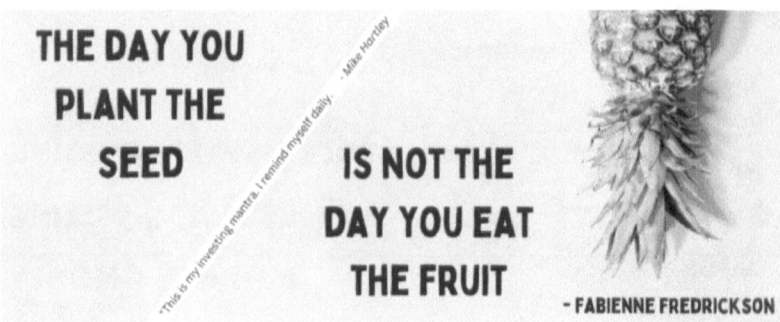

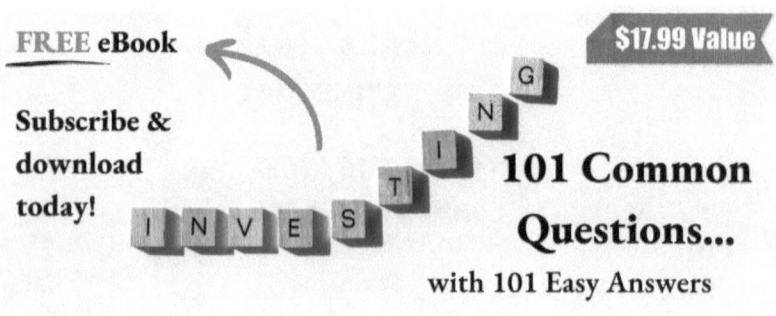

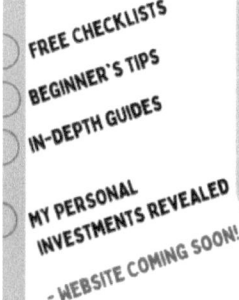

Subscribe To The Newsletter and Join Us!

- Find out the secrets to investing safely
- Join the growing **FIRE** (**F**inancially **I**ndependent **R**etire **E**arly) Movement!
- Live your passive income lifestyle…

www.thefirefund.com/free-gift

Mike Hartley

Table of Contents

Understanding the Stock Markets _____31

What Are the Different Types of Stocks and Shares I Can Invest In _____ 34

More Detailed Answers to Common Investing Questions

Understanding Stocks & Shares; Basics

Question 1 –What Is Investing?

Investing is the act of allocating resources, usually money, with the expectation of generating an additional income or profit.

Question 2 – What Is a Stock?

A stock also called a share, is a unit of ownership in a corporation. Stockholders are partial owners of the corporation and have a claim on the company's assets and profits. They may also vote on corporate matters. There are two types of stock: common and preferred. Common stock entitles the holder to vote at shareholder meetings and to receive dividends but does not guarantee these rights. Preferred stock entitles the holder to vote and to receive dividends at a fixed rate but does not generally give the holder an ownership stake in the company.

Question 3 – What Are Earnings?

Earnings are profits that a company generates from its business operations. They can be reported on a quarterly or annual basis. Earnings are substantial because they give investors an idea of a company's performance and whether its stock is undervalued or overvalued.

Question 4 – What Is a Dividend?

A dividend is a distribution of profits a company pays its shareholders. Dividends are important because they give investors a way to receive some of the profits they have earned from their investment in a company. Dividends are usually paid out every quarter. They can be in the form of cash or shares of stock.

Question 5 – What Is Stock Market Risk?

Risk is the chance that an investment will lose value. All investments carry some risk, but some are riskier than others. Riskier investments have the potential to generate higher returns, but they also come with a greater chance of loss.

Question 6 – What Is a Blue-Chip Stock?

A blue-chip stock is a stock that a well-established and financially sound company issues. They are often considered to be less risky than other types of stocks.

Question 7 – How Do I Buy Stocks?

You can buy stocks through a broker. A broker is a person or firm that buys and sells securities on behalf of clients. When you buy stocks, you're buying a piece of ownership in a public company.

Question 8 – What Is a Stockbroker?

As mentioned above, a stockbroker, or more simply a broker, is an individual or firm that buys and sells securities on behalf of its clients. Brokers make money by charging commissions on the trades that they execute.

Question 9 – What Is a Stock Portfolio?

A portfolio is a collection of investments, such as stocks, bonds, and mutual funds. Portfolios can be tailored to fit each investor's goals and risk tolerance.

Question 10 – What Is a Diversified Portfolio?

A diversified portfolio contains a mix of different investments, including stocks, bonds, commodities, and cash. Diversification aims to balance risk and return by investing in various assets that are not all influenced by the same factors. For example, if you invest only in stocks, you are taking on more risk than investing in a mix of stocks and bonds. But if you invest only in cash, you may miss out on potential returns. The key is finding the right asset mix for your circumstances.

There are many ways to diversify your portfolio, and no perfect formula exists. Some common approaches include investing in various asset classes in various geographical regions, and in a mix of companies of different sizes. Again, it is important to speak with a financial advisor before making any decisions about how to diversify your portfolio.

Question 11 – Why Is Diversification Important?

Diversification is important because it helps to minimize the effects of volatility and maximize returns. By investing in a variety of different asset classes, investors can protect themselves from losses in any one area.

Question 12 – How Can I Diversify My Portfolio?

There are several ways to diversify a portfolio, including investing in different asset classes, investing in different geographical regions, and investing in different types of securities.

Question 13 – What Is an Investment Bank?

An investment bank is a financial institution that underwrites and helps to sell new securities issues. Investment banks also provide other services, such as mergers and acquisitions advice and trading for their own account.

Question 14 – What Is a 401(K)?

A 401(k) is a retirement savings plan offered by many employers. Employees can choose to have a portion of their paycheck withheld and invested in a 401(k) account. Employers often match a portion of employee contributions.

Question 15 – What Is An IRA?

An IRA, or individual retirement account, is a personal investment account that offers tax advantages for retirement savings. There are several different types of IRAs, including traditional IRAs, Roth IRAs, and SEP IRAs.

Question 16 – Why Should I Invest or Save For Retirement?

There are several important reasons to start saving for retirement as early as possible. The sooner you start saving, the more time your money must grow. Even if you can only save a small amount each month, starting early will allow your savings to compound over time and give you a larger nest egg to retire on. In addition to giving your money more time to grow, starting to save early can also help reduce the effects of inflation. Over time, prices for goods and services tend to go up, which means that your money will not buy as much in the future as it does today. By starting to save now, you can help offset the effects of inflation and ensure that your retirement savings will last longer.

Question 17 – How Do I Know Which Stocks to Buy?

This is a difficult question to answer, as there are many factors to consider when making investment decisions. However, some resources can help, such as stock-picking services and financial news websites. The aim of this investment series is to provide you with some help with this question!

Question 18 – What Factors Should I Consider Before Investing?

The three main factors to consider before investing are:

- Your investment goals – What are you hoping to achieve by investing?

- Your risk tolerance – How much risk are you willing to take on?

- Your time horizon – When do you need or want the money back?

Question 19 – What Are Some Common Investment Terms?

Some common investment terms include:

- Asset allocation – The process of dividing an investment portfolio among different asset classes, in an effort to diversify risk.

- Diversification – A risk management technique that involves investing in a variety of assets in order to offset the risk posed by any one individual asset.

- Financial advisor – A professional who provides guidance and advice on personal finance matters, including investments, taxes, retirement planning, and estate planning.

- Investment portfolio – A collection of investments an individual or institution holds.

- Risk tolerance – The amount of risk an investor is willing to take on in pursuit of return.

- Stock – A type of security that represents ownership in a corporation.

- Volatility – A measure of the fluctuations in the price of a security over time. Higher volatility = higher risk.

Question 20 – What Is the Difference Between Investing and Speculation

Investing is the process of putting your money into assets that are expected to appreciate over time. Speculation is the process of making predictions about the future price movements of an asset, such as a stock or commodity.

Speculation is a riskier investment than investing, but it also has the potential for higher returns. Speaking with a financial advisor before deciding how to invest your money is important.

Question 21 – What Is Investing with Portfolio Volatility?

Portfolio volatility is a measure of how much the value of your portfolio fluctuates over time. A volatile portfolio experiences large swings in value, while a non-volatile portfolio experiences smaller swings.

Volatile portfolios can be risky than non-volatile portfolios, but they also offer the potential for higher returns. Speaking with a financial advisor before deciding how to invest your money is important.

Understanding the Stock Markets

Question 22 – What Is a Stock Market?

The stock market is a collection of markets where stocks (pieces of ownership in businesses) are traded between investors. It usually refers to the exchanges where stocks and other securities are bought and sold. The stock market can be used to measure the performance of a whole economy or sectors of it.

Question 23 – What Is the Dow Jones Industrial Average?

The Dow Jones Industrial Average (DJIA) is one of the most popular stock market indexes in the world. It is a price-weighted index, which means that the stocks with the highest prices have the largest impact on the index's movements. The DJIA is made up of 30 large, publicly owned companies from a variety of industries.

Question 24 – What Is The S&P 500?

The S&P 500 is another popular stock market index. It is a market-cap-weighted index, meaning that the companies with the largest market capitalizations (i.e., the most valuable companies) have the biggest impact on the index's movements. The S&P 500 is made up of 500 large, publicly owned companies from a variety of industries.

Question 25 – Why Are There Different Stock Markets?

There are different stock markets because companies choose to list their stocks on certain exchanges. For example, a company might list its stock on the New York Stock Exchange (NYSE) or the Nasdaq. Listing on a particular exchange may make the stock more attractive to certain investors.

Question 26 – What Is the Difference Between the NYSE and the Nasdaq?

The NYSE, or New York Stock Exchange, is a physical exchange where traders buy and sell stocks. The Nasdaq is an electronic exchange, and it is also the largest

exchange for tech stocks.

Question 27 – What Are 10 Examples of Stock Markets I Might Have Heard Of?

1. New York Stock Exchange (NYSE)

2. Nasdaq

3. London Stock Exchange (LSE)

4. Tokyo Stock Exchange (TSE)

5. Shanghai Stock Exchange (SSE)

6. Hong Kong Stock Exchange (HKEx)

7. Euronext

8. Australian Securities Exchange (ASX)

9. Toronto Stock Exchange (TSX)

10. Bombay Stock Exchange (BSE)

What Are the Different Types of Stocks and Shares I Can Invest In

Question 28 – What Are the Different Types Of 'Stocks'?

There are two main types of stocks: common stock and preferred stock. Common stock is the most common type of stock and gives investors voting rights and dividends. Preferred stock does not usually give investors voting rights, but it does come with preference regarding dividends and assets.

Question 29 – What Are the Different Types of Investments?

The three main categories of investments are:

- Cash and equivalents, which includes items such as savings accounts, certificates of deposit, and money market funds.

- Fixed-income securities, which include bonds and

other debt instruments.

- Equities, which include stocks and other ownership stakes in businesses.

Question 30 – What Is a Bond?

A bond is a debt security, like an IOU. When you buy a bond, you lend money to the issuer, usually a corporation or government. In return, the issuer promises to pay you interest and repay your loan when the bond matures. Bonds are often referred to as fixed-income securities because they pay a fixed interest rate.

Question 31 – What Is a Mutual Fund?

A mutual fund is a type of investment vehicle that pools money from many investors and invests it in a variety of assets, such as stocks, bonds, or short-term debt. Mutual funds are managed by professional money managers.

Question 32 – What Is a Growth Stock?

A growth stock is a stock that is issued by a company that is expected to experience above-average growth. Growth stocks are often more volatile than other types of stocks, but they can offer higher returns in the long run.

Question 33 – What Is a Value Stock?

A value stock is a stock that is issued by a company that appears to be undervalued by the market. Value investors believe that these stocks will eventually regain their true value and offer good returns.

Question 34 – What Is a Penny Stock?

A penny stock is a stock that trades for less than $5 per share. Penny stocks are often considered to be high risk because they are issued by small, unknown companies.

Question 35 – What Is an Index Fund?

An index fund is a type of investment fund that aims to track the performance of a specific market index, such as the S&P 500. Index funds are often used as a passive investing strategy.

Question 36 – What Is an ETF?

An ETF, or exchange-traded fund, is a type of investment vehicle that trades on a stock exchange. ETFs are like mutual funds, but they have some key differences. For one, ETFs are traded like stocks, so their prices can fluctuate throughout the day.

Additionally, ETFs often have lower fees than mutual funds.

Question 37 – What Is the Difference Between an Index Fund and an ETF?

An index fund is a type of mutual fund that tracks a specific market index, such as the S&P 500. An ETF is a type of security that tracks an underlying asset, such as a basket of commodities or a group of stocks.

Index funds typically have lower fees than ETFs but tend to have lower returns. ETFs can be more volatile than index funds, but they also offer the potential for higher returns. Speaking with a financial advisor before deciding how to invest your money is important.

Question 38 – What Is Meant by 'Investing with Currencies'?

Currencies are money that is used in different countries. They can be traded on exchanges, and they can be risky investments. Prices for currencies can be very volatile, and they are often influenced by factors such as economic conditions and political events.

Some investors choose to invest in currencies to diversify their portfolios and protect against inflation.

Others believe that currencies offer the potential for high returns, although this is not always the case. Speaking with a financial advisor before deciding how to invest your money is important.

Question 39 – What Is the Difference Between a Growth Stock and a Value Stock?

Growth stocks are companies that are expected to experience high growth rates. Value stocks are stocks of companies that are trading at a price that is below their intrinsic value.

Growth stocks can be a risky investment, but they also have the potential for high returns. Value stocks can offer investors the opportunity to buy a stock at a discount and realize a profit when the stock's price increases. Speaking with a financial advisor before deciding how to invest your money is important.

Question 40 – What Is the Difference Between an Index Fund and a Mutual Fund?

An index fund is a type of mutual fund that tracks a specific market index, such as the S&P 500. Index funds are passive investments, meaning they are not actively managed by a fund manager. Instead, they are designed to track the performance of the underlying index. Index funds typically have lower fees than actively managed mutual funds, and they can be a good option for investors who are looking for a simple, low-cost way to invest.

A mutual fund is an investment vehicle that allows investors to pool their money together and invest in a variety of assets, such as stocks, bonds, or cash. Mutual funds are actively managed by a fund manager, who makes decisions about which investments to buy and sell. Mutual funds typically have higher fees than index funds, but they can offer more diversification and professional management.

Question 41 – What Is the Difference Between a Stock and a Bond?

A stock is a type of security that represents ownership in a company. When you own a stock, you are entitled to a share of the profits or losses of the company. stocks can be bought and sold on exchanges, and they are typically used to raise capital for companies.

Bonds are another type of security that represents debt. When you buy a bond, you lend money to the issuer, such as a corporation or government. In return, the issuer agrees to pay you interest payments and to return your principal investment when the bond matures. Bonds can also be bought and sold on exchanges, and they are typically used by issuers to raise capital for their operations.

Question 42 – What Is Meant by 'Investing with Commodities'?

Commodities are raw materials that are used to produce goods and services. They include things like oil, gas, gold, and wheat. Commodities are traded on exchanges, and they can be risky investments. Prices for commodities can be very volatile, and they are often influenced by factors such as weather and political events.

Some investors choose to invest in commodities to diversify their portfolios and protect against inflation. Others believe that commodities offer the potential for high returns, although this is not always the case. Speaking with a financial advisor before deciding how to invest your money is important.

Question 43 – What Is Meant by 'Dividend Investing'?

Dividend investing is the process of investing in stocks that pay dividends. Dividends are payments made by companies to their shareholders, and they can be a great way to earn income from your investments.

Dividend investing can be a riskier investment than some other types of investments, but it also has the potential for higher returns. It is important to speak with a financial advisor before deciding how to invest your money.

Question 44 – What Is Meant by a 'Dividend Yield'?

A dividend yield is the percentage of a stock's price that is paid out in dividends. For example, if a stock has a dividend yield of 2%, that means that for every $100 you invest in the stock, you will receive $2 in dividends.

Dividend yields can vary widely and can be a great way to generate income from your investments. It is important to speak with a financial advisor before deciding how to invest your money.

Question 45 – What Is Meant by a 'Dividend Date'?

Dividend dates are the dates on which companies pay their shareholders dividends. These payments can be a great way to generate income from your investments.

Dividend dates can vary widely, so it is important to speak with a financial advisor before making any decisions about how to invest your money.

Question 46 – What Is Meant by A 'Retirement Plan'?

Dividend ReInvestment Plans (or DRIPs) allow shareholders to reinvest their dividends into the company. This can be a great way to grow your investment over time.

DRIPs can be riskier than other types of investments, but they also offer the potential for higher returns. It is important to speak with a financial advisor before deciding how to invest your money.

Understanding Stocks & Shares; Intermediate

Question 47 – What Is a Stock Split?

A stock split is when a company increases the number of shares that it has outstanding. This is usually done to make the stock more affordable for small investors. A stock split does not change the value of a company.

Question 48 – What Is Market Capitalization?

Market capitalization is the value of a company's shares of stock outstanding multiplied by the current market price per share. It is often used as a rough measure of a company's size.

Question 49 – What Is a Bull Market?

A bull market is a period in which stock prices are rising and optimistic investor sentiment prevails. Bull markets are often characterized by strong economic growth and low levels of unemployment.

Question 50 – What Is a Bear Market?

A bear market is the opposite of a bull market, characterized by falling stock prices and negative investor sentiment. Bear markets are often caused by economic recession or uncertainty.

Question 51 – What Is a Hedge Fund?

A hedge fund is an investment fund that employs aggressive strategies to make high returns, such as leverage and short selling. Hedge funds are only available to accredited investors with a high net worth.

Question 52 – What Are Some Common Investment Strategies?

Some common investment strategies include:

- **Buy and hold** – A strategy in which an investor buys a security and holds it for a long period of time, regardless of market conditions.

- **Dollar-cost averaging** – A strategy in which an

investor buys a fixed dollar amount of a security at fixed intervals, regardless of the price. The goal is to reduce the effects of volatility by buying more shares when prices are low and fewer shares when prices are high.

- **Value investing** – A strategy in which an investor looks for securities that are trading at a discount to their intrinsic value.

- **Growth investing** – A strategy in which an investor looks for securities with the potential to experience above-average growth.

- **Income investing** – A strategy in which an investor looks for securities that offer a high yield.

These are just a few basic strategies that you may want to consider. Investors can take many other approaches, and the right strategy for you will depend on your circumstances. Speaking with a financial advisor before making any investment decisions is important.

Question 53 - What Is Active Investing?

Active investing is a style of investing in which the investor takes a more hands-on approach, making decisions about individual investments and actively managing their portfolio.

Question 54 - What Is Passive Investing?

Passive investing is a style of investing in which the investor takes a more hands-off approach, opting to invest in a broad market index or using other pre-determined investment strategies.

Question 55 - What Are the Advantages and Disadvantages of Active Investing?

The advantages of active investing include the ability to tailor a portfolio to specific goals, the potential to outperform the market, and the opportunity to generate income through dividends and other distributions. The disadvantages of active investing include the higher costs associated with transactional activity, the time commitment required to research investments, and the greater risk of underperforming the market.

Question 56 – What Are the Advantages and Disadvantages of Passive Investing?

The advantages of passive investing include lower costs, simplicity, and greater diversification. The disadvantages of passive investing include the potential to underperform the market and a lack of control over individual investments.

Question 57 – What Is an Asset Class?

An asset class is a group of securities that share similar characteristics. The three main asset classes are:

- Cash and equivalents

- Fixed-income securities

- Equities

Question 58 – What Are the Different Types of Assets?

There are four major asset classes: stocks, bonds, commodities, and cash. Each asset class has its own characteristics and risks. For example, stocks tend to be more volatile than bonds but offer the potential for higher returns. Commodities are often seen as a hedge against inflation, as their prices increase when the cost-of-living increases. Cash is the least risky asset class but also offers the lowest potential return.

Now that you know some of the basics of investing, you can start to think about which asset class or classes are right for you. Remember to always consult with a financial advisor before making any investment decisions.

Question 59 – So, What Is Asset Allocation, and How Does It Work with Investing?

Asset allocation is the process of dividing your investment portfolio among different asset classes. The goal of asset allocation is to balance risk and return so that your portfolio is diversified, and you are not overexposed to any one type of investment. For example, if you put all your money into stocks, you are taking on more risk than investing in a mix of stocks and bonds. But if you invest only in cash, you may miss out on potential returns. The key is finding the right asset mix for your circumstances.

There are many ways to allocate your assets, and no perfect formula exists. Some common approaches include equal weighting, where each asset class makes up an equal portion of your portfolio; strategic asset allocation, where you make choices based on your investment goals; and dynamic asset allocation, where you adjust your holdings as market conditions change. Again, it is important to speak with a financial advisor before deciding how to allocate your assets.

Question 60 – What Is a Security?

A security is a financial instrument that represents an ownership stake in a company or debt obligation of a government or corporation. Examples of securities include stocks, bonds, and mutual funds.

Question 61 – What Is Meant by Horizontal Diversification?

Horizontal diversification is a strategy whereby an investor spreads their investment across several different companies in the same industry. This is often done to mitigate risk; if one company in the industry experiences difficulties, the others may offset any losses.

Question 62 – What Are Blue Chip Stocks?

Blue chip stocks are those issued by large, well-established companies with a strong performance history. They are often seen as a safe investment, as these companies are typically less volatile than smaller companies.

Question 63 – What Are Small Chip Stocks?

Small-cap stocks are issued by smaller companies that tend to be more volatile than blue chips. They often offer higher potential returns but come with a greater degree of risk.

Question 64 – What Is Meant by Vertical Diversification?

Vertical diversification is a strategy that involves investing in a variety of assets that are not all influenced by the same factors. For example, if you invest only in stocks, you are taking on more risk than investing in a mix of stocks and bonds. But if you invest only in cash, you may miss out on potential returns. The key is finding the right asset mix for your circumstances.

There are many ways to diversify your portfolio, and no perfect formula exists. Some common approaches include investing in various asset classes, in various geographical regions and in a mix of companies of different sizes. Again, it is important to speak with a financial advisor before deciding how to invest your money.

Question 65 – What Is Unsystematic Risk and Systematic Risk?

Unsystematic risk is specific to a particular company or industry and can be mitigated through diversification. Systematic risk is inherent in the market as a whole and cannot be diversified away. Examples of systematic risk include economic recessions and geopolitical unrest.

Question 66 – What Is the Difference Between Fundamental Analysis and Technical Analysis When Investing?

Fundamental analysis is a stock selection method that looks at a company's financial statements and other factors to determine its intrinsic value. Technical analysis is a stock selection method that looks at past price patterns to predict future price movements.

Both methods have pros and cons, and neither guarantees success. Many investors use a combination of both methods when making investment decisions. Speaking with a financial advisor before deciding how to invest your money is important.

Question 67 – What Is Strategic Diversification?

Strategic diversification is an investment strategy that involves spreading your money across various asset classes to minimize risk. This strategy can be used when investing in stocks, bonds, and other types of assets.

Diversifying your portfolio can help protect you from losses if one asset class falls in value. However, it is important to remember that no investment is completely risk-free. Speaking with a financial advisor before deciding how to invest your money is important.

Question 68 – What Are the Risks and Rewards of Investing in Real Estate?

Real estate investing can be a great way to build wealth over time. However, there are some risks associated with this type of investment. For example, the value of your property could go down if the local market experiences a downturn.

Real estate investing can be a riskier investment than some other types of investments, but it also has the potential for higher returns. Speaking with a financial advisor before deciding how to invest your money is important.

Question 69 – What Are the Risks and Rewards of Investing in Foreign Markets?

Foreign markets can be volatile, but they also offer the potential for high returns. These markets can be riskier than domestic markets, so it is important to speak with a financial advisor before making any decisions about how to invest your money.

Question 70 –What Is Investing with Buybacks?

Stock buybacks are when companies buy back their own stock from investors. This can be a great way to return money to shareholders, and it can also help boost the stock's value.

Buybacks can also be riskier than some other types of investments, but they also offer the potential for higher returns. It is important to speak with a financial advisor before deciding how to invest your money.

Question 71 – What Are ETFs Vs ETNs?

ETFs and ETNs are both types of investment products that trade on exchanges. ETFs are Exchange Traded Funds, and they are a type of investment product that holds a basket of assets. ETNs are Exchange Traded Notes, and they are a type of debt security.

Question 72 – What Are Stop Losses / Stop Orders?

Stop losses are an order that is placed with a broker to sell a security when it reaches a certain price. This is done to limit losses on an investment.

Stop losses can be a great way to protect your investments but can also limit your potential profits. Speaking with a financial advisor before deciding how to invest your money is important.

Question 73 – What Is a Limit Order?

A limit order is buying or selling a security at a certain price. This is done in order to get the best possible price for the security.

Limit orders can be a great way to get the best possible price for your investment, but they can also limit your potential profits.

Question 74 – What Is a Market Order?

A market order is buying or selling a security at the current market price. This is the most basic type of order, and it will fill at the best available price.

Market orders are a great way to fill your trade quickly, but they can limit your potential profits. It is important to speak with a financial advisor before deciding how to invest your money.

Question 75 – What Is a Trailing Stop Limit Order?

A trailing stop limit order is an order to buy or sell a security when it reaches a certain price. This is done to limit losses on an investment. The stop price is set at a certain percentage below the market price, and the order will only fill if the security reaches that price.

Appreciating Risk and Things to Avoid with the Stock Market

Question 76 – What Are Some Risks Associated with Buying Stocks?

There are several risks associated with buying stocks, including market, credit, and liquidity risks. Market risk is the risk that the value of your investment will go down due to changes in the overall market. The biggest risk of investing in stocks is that the value of the stock can go down, which would result in a loss for the investor. There is also the risk that the company whose stock is being bought could go bankrupt, which would also lead to a significant loss.

Question 77 – What Is Insider Trading?

Insider trading is the illegal practice of buying or selling security based on material, non-public information. It is illegal because it gives some investors an unfair advantage over others.

Question 78 – What Are Some Common Investment Mistakes?

Some common investment mistakes include:

- Investing without a plan

- Chasing after hot stocks

- Trying to time the market

- Failing to diversify

- Relying on emotion instead of data

Question 79 – What Are Some Common Pitfalls to Avoid When Investing?

Investors should avoid several common pitfalls, including chasing performance, letting emotions guide decisions, and failing to diversify. When you chase performance, you try to buy investments that have done well in the past in the hope that they will continue to do well in the future. But this approach is often unsuccessful, as it is difficult to predict which investments will be successful over the long term. Instead of chasing performance, it is important to develop and stick to a sound investment strategy.

Similarly, letting emotions guide investment decisions is often a recipe for disaster. If you make decisions based on fear or greed, you are more likely to make impulsive choices that are not in your best interest. It is important to stay disciplined and focused on your long-term goals.

Finally, failing to diversify is another common mistake that investors make. When you fail to diversify, you essentially put all your eggs in one basket. This approach increases your risk, as you rely on a single investment to perform well. Instead, you should diversify your portfolio to balance risk and return.

These are just a few of the most common pitfalls to avoid when investing. Investors can make many other mistakes, so it is important to speak with a financial advisor before deciding how to invest your money.

Understanding Stocks & Shares; Advanced

Question 80 – What Is an IPO?

An IPO, or initial public offering, is when a company first sells shares of stock to the public. IPOs are often accompanied by a great deal of media hype and can be risky investments since there is no track record to assess how well the company will perform as a publicly traded entity.

Question 81 – What Are Correlation Charts?

A correlation chart is a tool that investors use to visualize the relationship between two variables. For example, one might create a correlation chart to compare the stock prices of two companies. If the stock prices move in the same direction (i.e., they are positively correlated), then the companies will likely be in the same industry and influenced by the same factors. If the stock prices move in opposite directions (i.e., they are negatively correlated), then the companies will likely be in different industries and influenced by different factors. Correlation charts can be used to spot relationships between stocks, commodities, currencies, etc.

Question 82 – What Is Beta Correlation?

Beta correlation is a measure of the relationship between two variables. In finance, beta is often used to measure the volatility of a stock in relation to the market. A stock with a high beta is more volatile than the market, while a stock with a low beta is less volatile. Beta correlation can be used to spot relationships between stocks, commodities, currencies, etc.

Question 83 – What Is a Stock Split?

A stock split is when a company divides its existing shares into multiple new shares. This has the effect of reducing the price of each share, making it more affordable for investors.

Question 84 – What Is a Stock Dividend?

A stock dividend is when a company issues new shares to shareholders to distribute its profits. This has the effect of diluting the ownership stake of each shareholder but typically also increases the share price.

Question 85 – What Is the Difference Between Buying a Stock and Shorting a Stock?

When you buy a stock, you are buying shares of a company that you expect will increase in value. When you short a stock, you are selling shares of a company that you expect will decrease in value.

Shorting a stock is a riskier investment than buying one, but it also has the potential for higher returns. It is important to speak with a financial advisor before deciding how to invest your money.

Question 86 – What Are the Risks and Rewards of Investing In Penny Stocks?

Penny stocks are low-priced shares of companies that are typically not well-known. These stocks can be volatile and risky, but they also offer the potential for high returns.

Penny stocks are speculative investments, and they should only be purchased by investors who are willing to take on a high level of risk. It is important to speak with a financial advisor before making any decisions about how to invest your money.

Question 87 – What Are the Risks and Rewards Of Investing In Precious Metals?

Precious metals can be a volatile investment, but they also offer the potential for high returns. These investments can be riskier than some other types of investments, so it is important to take care, particularly if investing directly in precious metals directly rather than in an ETF structure.

Question 88 – What Is a Margin Order?

A margin order is buying or selling a security using borrowed money. This can be a great way to increase your potential profits, but it can also increase your risk.

Margin orders can greatly increase your potential profits, but they can also increase your risk. It is important to speak with a financial advisor before deciding how to invest your money.

Question 89 – What Is a Short Sell Order?

A short sell order is an order to sell a security that you do not own. This can be a great way to make profits if the security price goes down, but it can also be very risky.

Short-sell orders can be a great way to make profits if the price of the security goes down, but they can also be very risky. It is important to speak with a financial advisor before making any investment decisions about short selling.

Question 90 – What Are Inverse ETFs?

Inverse ETFs are a type of investment product designed to profit from a decline in the underlying asset's price. These products are typically used by investors who are bearish on the market or who want to hedge their portfolios.

Question 91 – What Are Leveraged ETFs?

Leveraged ETFs are a type of investment product that is designed to provide exposure to an asset with a higher degree of risk. These products are typically used by investors who are looking for a higher degree of return.

Question 92 – Can I Trade When the Markets Are Closed or Shut Down?

In the USA, investing in stocks and shares can be done

when markets are closed or shut down, although the opportunities for trading may be limited. The easy answer to this question would really be a clear 'no', not for the average investor; however, there are some situations where this isn't quite true. Let me explain.

When a market is closed or suspended due to extraordinary events such as natural disasters, government shutdowns, or extreme volatility in the market, trading activity may be halted temporarily. Depending on the severity of the situation, some exchanges may close earlier than expected or reopen later than expected.

When markets are closed, investors typically have access to their accounts but cannot place any new orders until the exchange reopens. Any existing open orders will remain in effect until they are either fulfilled or cancelled by their owners. It is also important to note that while a market may be closed in one area of the world due to different time zones and local regulations, it could still be open and available for trading elsewhere.

During these times of market closure and disruption, investors have several tools at their disposal to help them stay informed regarding current and future market conditions and maintain their financial portfolios. For example, live news feeds from media outlets can provide updated information about current events that could impact future stock prices. Additionally, using technical analysis can offer insight into potential trends that could influence a certain stock's performance during closures or disruptions.

Finally, investors should understand the risks of investing when markets are closed or shut down. Market makers often adjust prices in response to geopolitical events, which can cause significant price swings leading up to and following closures and suspensions; this means buying low or selling high might not always yield positive results for investors who jump into trades without appropriate research beforehand. Additionally, delayed order execution caused by an exchange's temporary closure can lead to missed opportunities if an investor's desired transaction isn't completed before a market reopens again at a higher price point than expected.

Question 93 – Is It Safe for Me to Invest In Unlisted Stocks?

It depends on your goals and risk profile as an investor. Unlisted stocks can offer great potential rewards, but they may also be subject to higher levels of risk than publicly traded stocks. As a beginner, it's wise to do your research and understand the associated risks before investing in unlisted stocks. Additionally, you should diversify your investments and spread the risk across multiple asset classes.

More Detailed Answers to Common Investing Questions

Question 94 – Should I Diversify My Stocks or Stick with One Really Solid Company Like Microsoft, Coca-Cola, Etc?

It is generally wise for investors to diversify their stock portfolio rather than putting all of their eggs in one basket. Having a diverse portfolio can be beneficial as it can help to reduce risk and increase potential returns. Holding stocks of just one company can provide significant exposure to the performance of that organization – and if that company's performance falters, your entire portfolio will suffer.

However, while diversification is typically seen as the best approach when investing in the stock market, there are some cases were focusing on a single solid company may make sense. For example, if you are confident in the company's prospects over time, it could make sense to concentrate your holdings in that business as a long-term bet. Companies like Microsoft and Coca-Cola have been around for decades and have consistently delivered strong returns to shareholders over that time – so they might be attractive investments for those looking for steady growth over the long haul.

Diversifying your stock holdings also means spreading out your risk across different sectors – such as tech, retail, healthcare, or finance – so that if one sector takes a hit from an economic crisis or another unforeseen event you don't take too much of a hit in your portfolio. This allows you to benefit from potential gains in multiple sectors at once and provides some protection against losses due to unforeseen events impacting any given sector at any given time.

Finally, diversifying across different countries is another way investors can mitigate risk while still achieving strong returns. Investing in international stocks can help smooth out volatility by providing broader access to markets with different economic cycles than you may find domestically. International stocks may also offer additional opportunities due to foreign exchange rate fluctuations between currencies, potentially giving you higher returns on your investments over the longer term.

In conclusion, while it may be tempting to focus solely on one solid company like Microsoft or Coca-Cola when investing in stocks and shares – diversifying across multiple companies and even countries may ultimately provide better protection from market downturns while still allowing investors access to potential gains from different sectors within the stock market. Taking a balanced approach through diversification could be the best way for most individual investors looking for steady growth over time without exposing themselves too heavily to any single company or sector of the market.

Question 95 – How Often Should I Rebalance My Portfolio of Stocks and Shares?

It depends on your individual goals and risk tolerance, but a good guideline is to rebalance your portfolio at least once a year. This will help ensure that you are not overly exposed to any particular stocks or shares and that your investments remain aligned with your long-term goals. It's also important to keep an eye on the markets throughout the year and make adjustments if certain stocks or sectors have taken off or if there has been unexpected price volatility.

Rebalancing your portfolio of stocks and shares should be done on a regular basis, typically every 6 months to 1 year. This allows you to ensure that the stocks and shares you invest in meet your investment goals and objectives. It also offers an opportunity to reallocate funds into different investments while taking advantage of market movements or economic changes. Rebalancing is important for managing risk, especially during volatile times in the stock market.

Question 96 – How Can Investors Capitalize on Fluctuations in The Stock Market?

Investors can capitalize on fluctuations in the stock market by taking advantage of short-term opportunities and trends. This could include buying and selling stocks quickly or pursuing arbitrage opportunities when the price of a stock deviates from its fair value. Investors should also be vigilant to spot trends in the overall market and individual sectors or industries that may arise due to economic or political news.

It is important to research what types of investments are likely to yield higher returns. For example, some investors may focus on penny stocks, which tend to be more volatile but offer greater potential gains than blue chip stocks. Other investors might look for companies with strong fundamentals that are not currently popular among investors but have the potential for growth. Investors can take advantage of these opportunities when they arise by staying vigilant and up to date on the latest news and earnings reports.

It is also important for investors to understand different strategies for managing risk when trying to capitalize on stock market fluctuations. One strategy could be deploying stop-loss orders, allowing investors to sell their stocks at a predetermined price if it decreases below a certain threshold. Additionally, investors should familiarize themselves with portfolio diversification and position sizing techniques to manage their risk while still enjoying the potential rewards of trading stocks.

Finally, investors should stay informed of any changes in legislation or regulations that could affect their investments in the stock market. For example, many countries levy taxes on certain types of investment income, so it is important for investors to be aware of any tax implications before investing their money into stocks and shares. By staying updated with all relevant information about the stock market, including both short-term trends and long-term factors affecting the markets, investors can make well-informed decisions about where and how much money they invest to maximize returns while minimizing risk.

Question 97 – How Much Money Do I Need to Start Investing With?

Investing in stocks, shares and funds can be a great way to build wealth, but it is important to understand how much money is needed to do so successfully. It's best to have at least $500 available to start investing. This amount is enough to diversify your portfolio to minimize risk and maximize returns. Having more capital gives you more flexibility when investing, allowing you to purchase more assets if desired. Additionally, having more money available helps reduce the cost of making trades since many brokers charge a fee per trade.

Furthermore, while some online brokerages may not require much upfront capital, they will typically require you to maintain a minimum balance or meet certain other requirements for them to cover the costs associated with processing your orders. It is essential that you understand the terms of any brokerage account before investing, as these requirements can vary greatly from one broker to another.

Finally, it is important for all investors to remember that stocks are not like savings accounts and can result in a loss of principal if not managed properly. As such, it pays off for investors who take the time to educate themselves about the risks associated with investing and develop an appropriate strategy for their investment goals. While building up enough capital for successful stock trading takes time and patience, taking the initiative will pay off handsomely in the long run.

Question 98 – What Are Some Reliable Resources for Getting Up To Date Market News and Analysis?

One reliable resource for getting up-to-date market news and analysis is investing websites such as Yahoo! Finance, Investopedia, and Seeking Alpha. These sites provide comprehensive market data and insights from experts in the field, such as stock performance summaries, earnings reports, analyst ratings, IPO information, financial statements and more. Additionally, these resources offer real-time updates on the performance of stocks, indices, and other investment instruments so that users can stay informed about their investments.

Other helpful resources include Bloomberg Businessweek for detailed economic analysis of markets across the world; Morningstar for mutual fund and ETF information; Motley Fool for in-depth research on individual stocks; Google Finance for streaming quotes and news; CNBC's website for industry news; and The Wall Street Journal's MarketBeat blog for up-to-date commentary on the stock market. It is important to note that some of these sites may require a subscription or paid access to view certain content. Additionally, investors should still exercise caution when researching online resources as there are many unreliable sources that could offer inaccurate or outdated information.

Question 99 – How Do I Analyze a Stock's Performance?

Analyzing a stock's performance is an essential step in investing. It involves looking at the current financial status of a company, as well as predicting future trends.

This analysis can help investors decide whether to buy, hold or sell a particular stock.

When analyzing the performance of a stock, investors should look for information such as the company's current financial health, its business model, competitors, and potential growth opportunities. Important indicators of a company's financial health include its revenues and earnings per share. Investors should also analyze the company's cash flow position and balance sheet to assess its ability to meet debt obligations. Investors must also consider the sector in which the company operates and any expected changes in industry dynamics that could affect the company's prospects.

Technical analysis is another important tool used to analyze stocks. Technical analysis helps investors identify patterns in historical data that can provide clues about how a stock might move in the near-term future. Popular technical indicators include moving averages, momentum indicators, trading volume and relative strength index (RSI). Investors can create a more well-rounded investment strategy by combining technical tools with fundamental analysis.

In addition to analyzing past performance, investors must also make predictions about how a stock will perform going forward. Analysts make use of various techniques such as comparison methods or multiples like price-earnings ratio (P/E), dividend yield or enterprise value-EBITDA multiple, discounted cash flow models, and relative valuation methods like peer-to-peer comparison to predict future returns on investment.

Overall, analyzing stocks before investing is an important step for all investors. Doing so provides insight into the past performance of a security while helping investors identify potential growth opportunities and risks associated with investing in it. With careful analysis of fundamental and technical factors and forecasting future trends, investors can make informed decisions when investing in individual stocks or even entire markets.

Question 100 – In the US, What Taxes Will I Pay on My Stocks and Shares Investments?

There are a variety of taxes that you may be liable to pay on your stocks and shares investments. For example, if you earn dividends from investment in stocks, you may be liable for federal income tax. Long-term capital gains (held for one year or more) are generally taxed lower than ordinary income and short-term capital gains (held for less than one year). In addition, some states impose their own taxes on dividend earnings or capital gains.

It's also important to note that you may be subject to taxation on a stock sale. This applies even if you do not receive any cash proceeds from the sale - such as when you gift or sell shares at a loss. Depending on your individual circumstances, it is possible for the proceeds of such a sale to be subject to federal capital gains tax, state taxes, and even alternative minimum tax (AMT).

One way in which investors can reduce their overall tax liability is by utilizing investments with qualified dividends. These are essentially corporate profits that have been taxed at the company level before they are distributed to shareholders as earnings. By taking advantage of these opportunities, investors can enjoy more advantageous tax rates when filing their returns with the IRS. Additionally, retirement accounts such as an IRA or 401(k) provide a layer of tax deferral and could help reduce taxable income.

It's important to remember that while planning an investment strategy with taxes in mind is important, it should not always be the determining factor when deciding what stocks and funds to buy and when. Taxes should only ever come secondary after careful consideration has been given regarding potential investments and associated risks.

Question 101 – How Can I Protect Myself from Losses When Investing?

Investing in stocks and shares can greatly increase your wealth, but it's important to understand the risk involved. You should always do your research before investing and have a plan in place to mitigate losses. There are several ways to protect yourself when investing in stocks and shares.

First, diversification is key. By spreading your investments across different sectors, you can reduce risk while still having the opportunity to earn returns potentially. This helps ensure that if one sector experiences losses, the others may help offset any losses experienced by that particular sector. Creating an asset allocation strategy appropriate for your goals and risk tolerance is also important.

Second, it's wise to set stop-loss orders with your broker so that you don't lose more than you can afford if a stock declines quickly. You should also limit margin trading as much as possible – using borrowed money to purchase securities increases the risk significantly.

Third, be sure to monitor your investments closely when they are held for a long period of time or purchased at high prices. If there is a significant decrease in their value, it may be wise to sell them and take the loss instead of possibly waiting for them to recover back up. Also, establishing time frames for specific trades can help you make well-informed decisions about when to exit a trade or adjust your position for potential gains or losses.

Finally, it's essential that you stay up to date on market news and analysis by utilizing reliable resources such as financial websites, books written by professional investors, and newsletters from experienced traders and investment advisors who specialize in stocks and shares – this will help you make informed decisions regarding when and how best to invest. By following these tips, investors can reduce their loss exposure while taking advantage of the potential returns associated with investing in stocks and shares.